Clever Happy

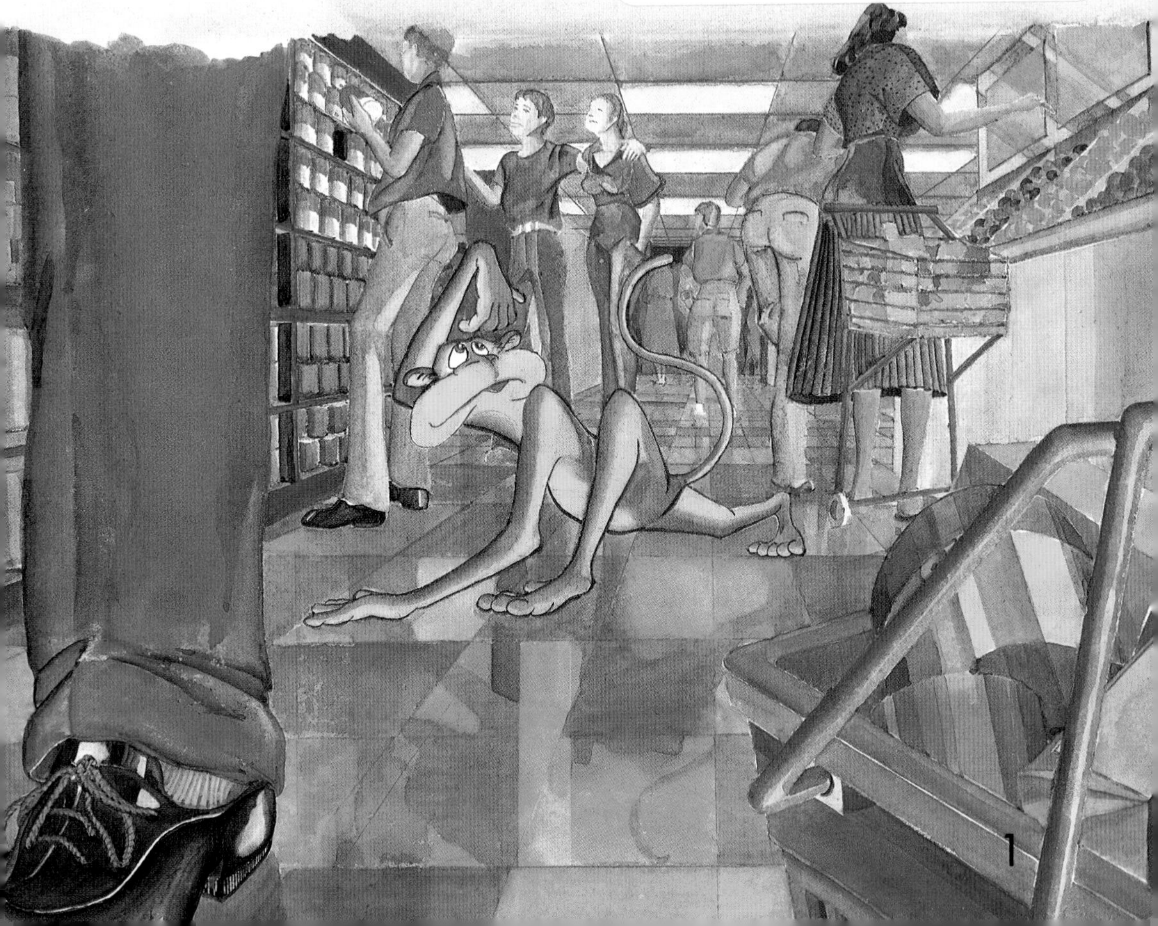

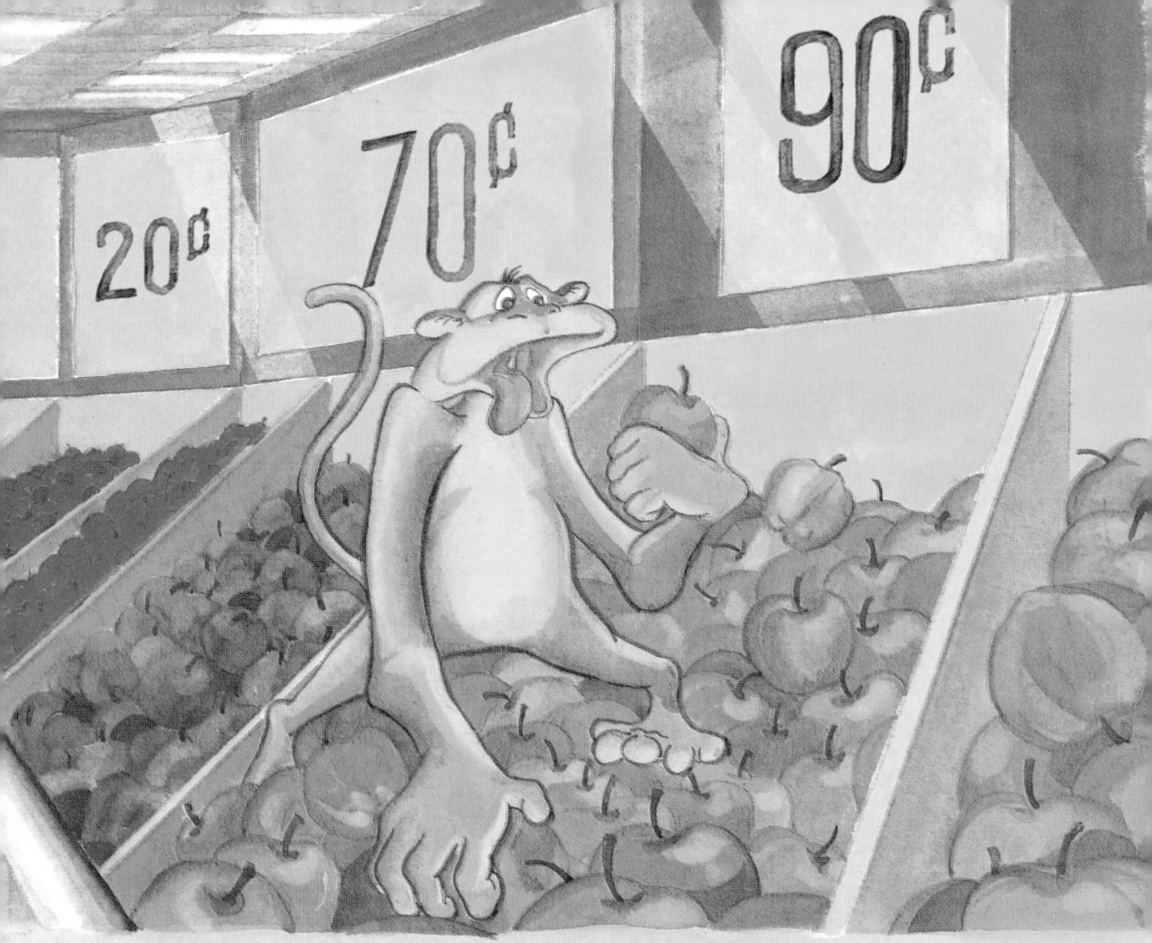

Happy has an apple.

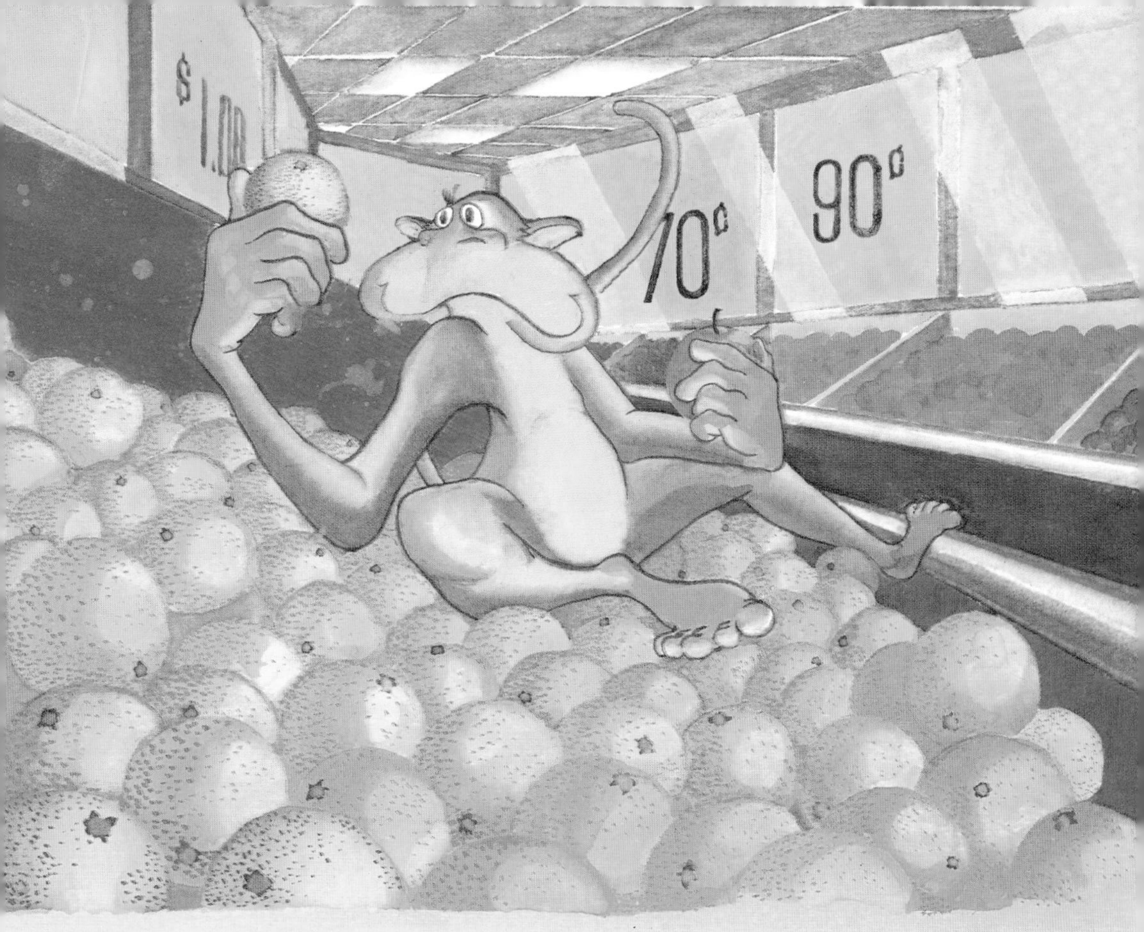

Happy has an orange.

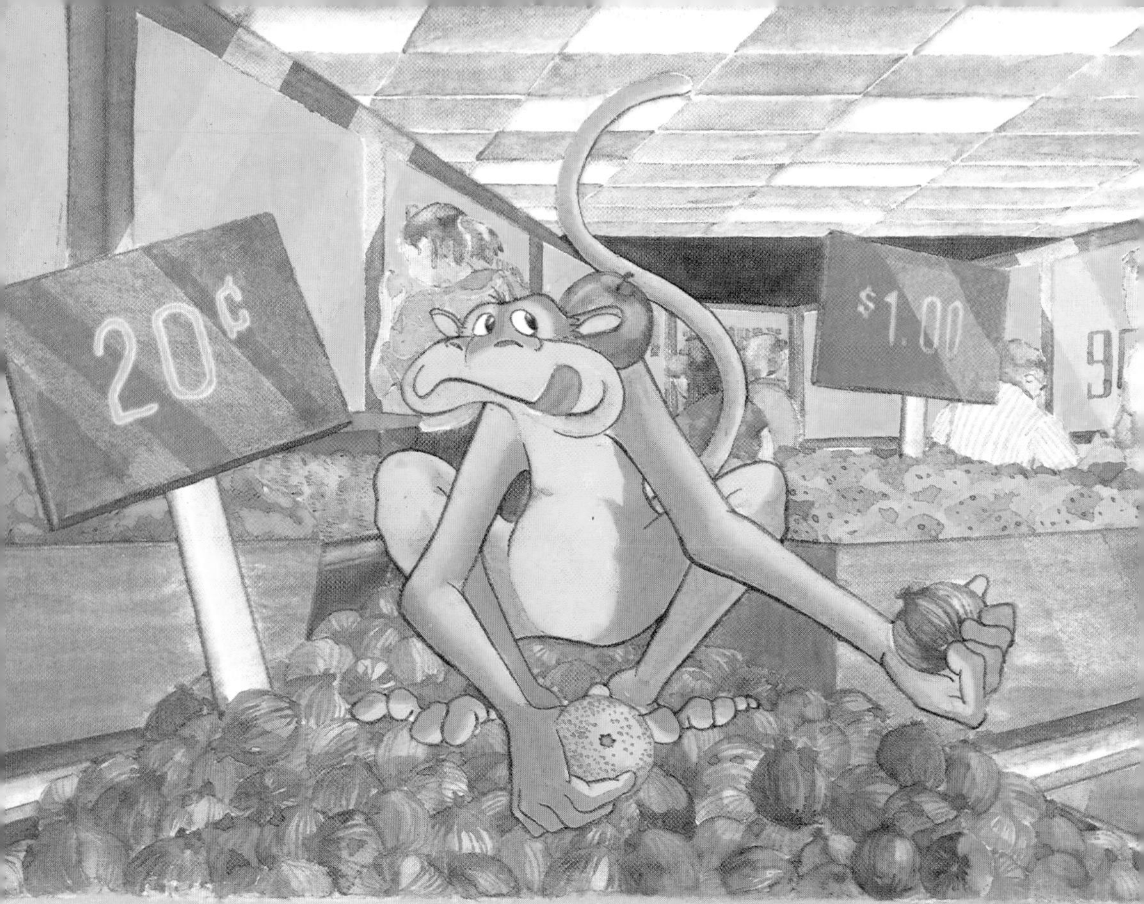

Happy has an onion.

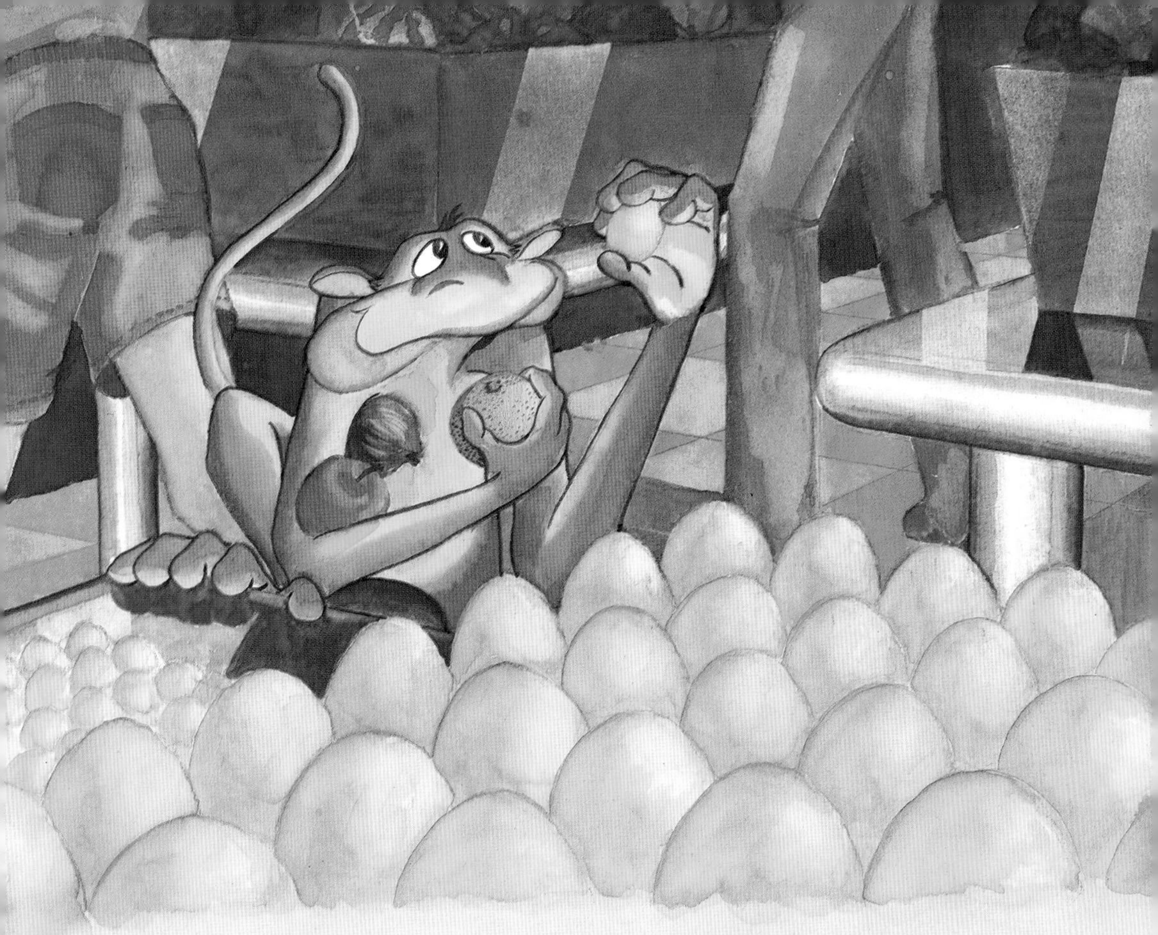

Happy has an egg.

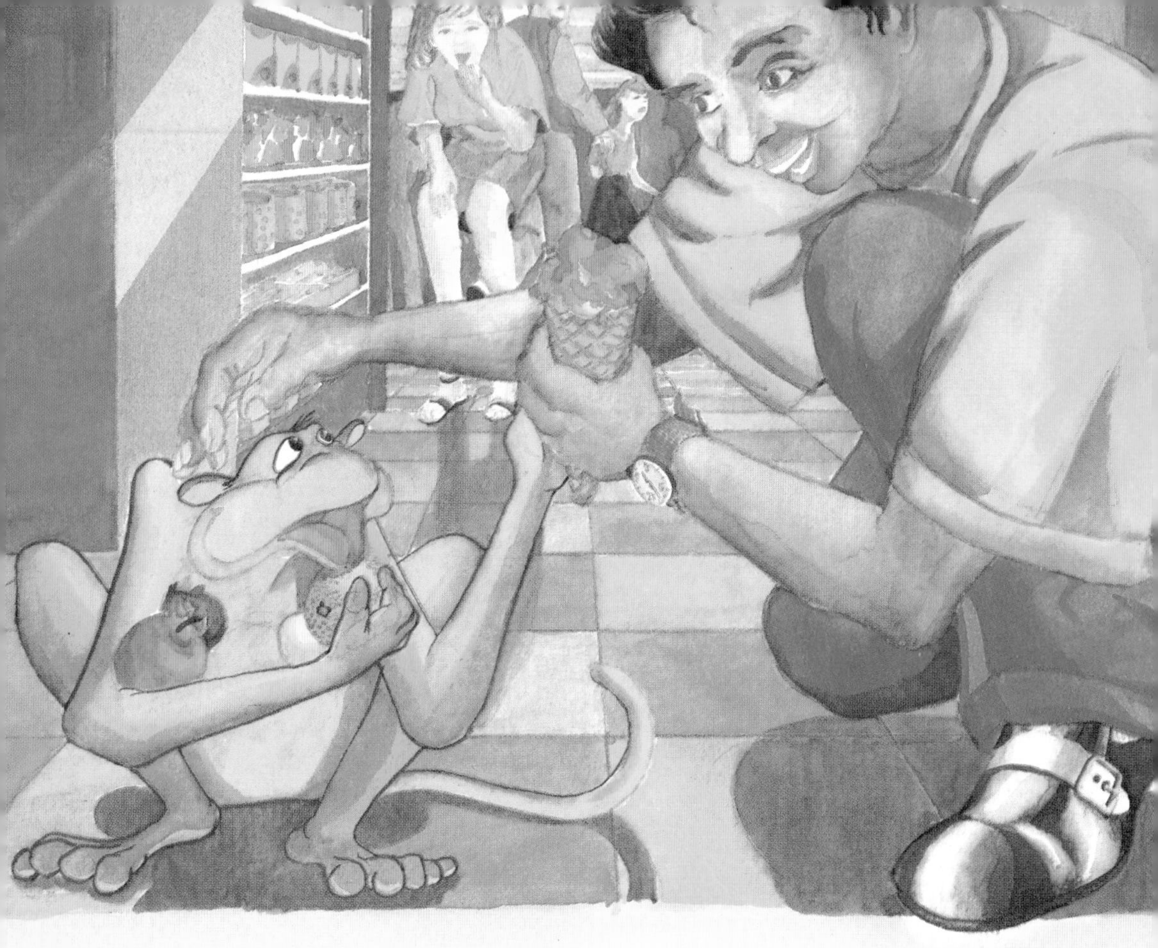

Happy has an ice-cream cone.

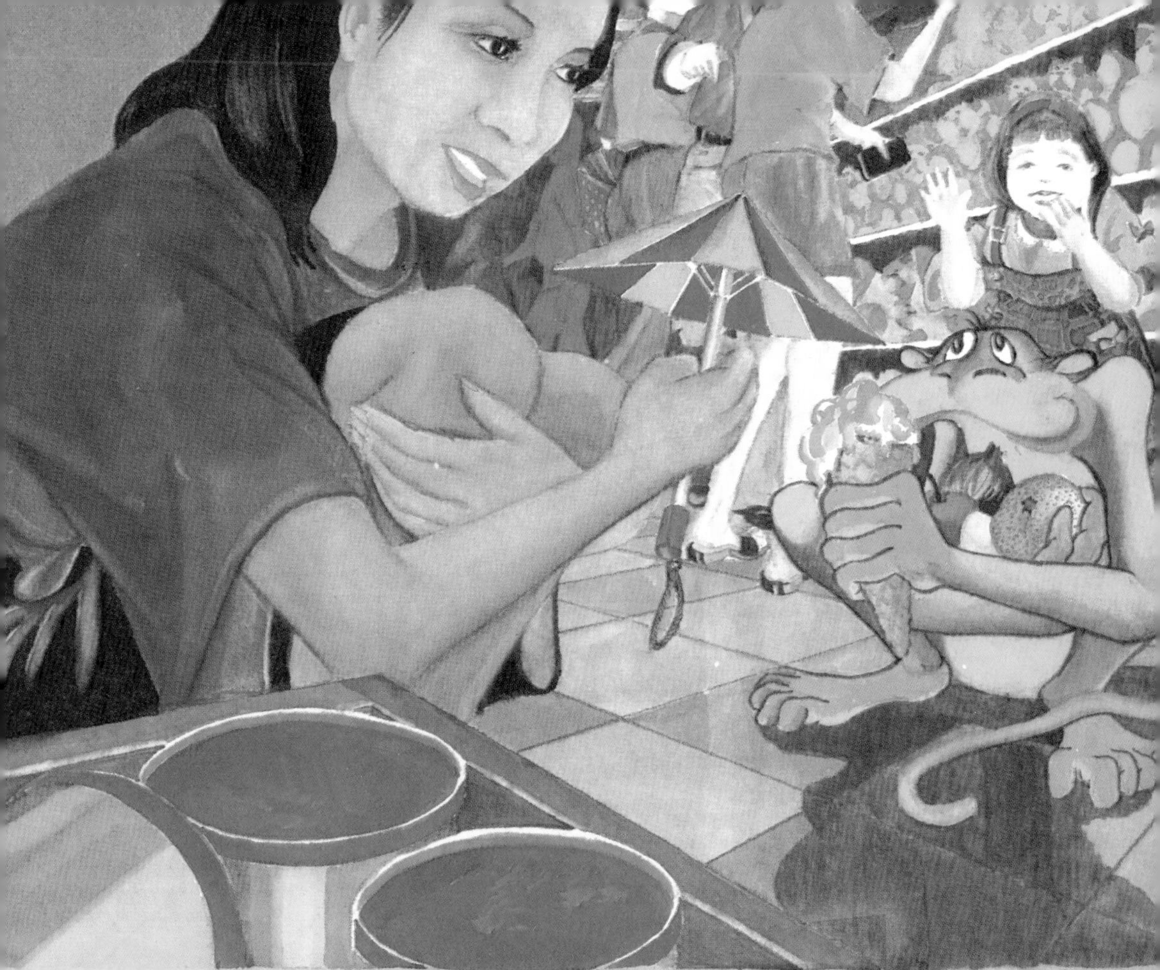

Happy has an umbrella.

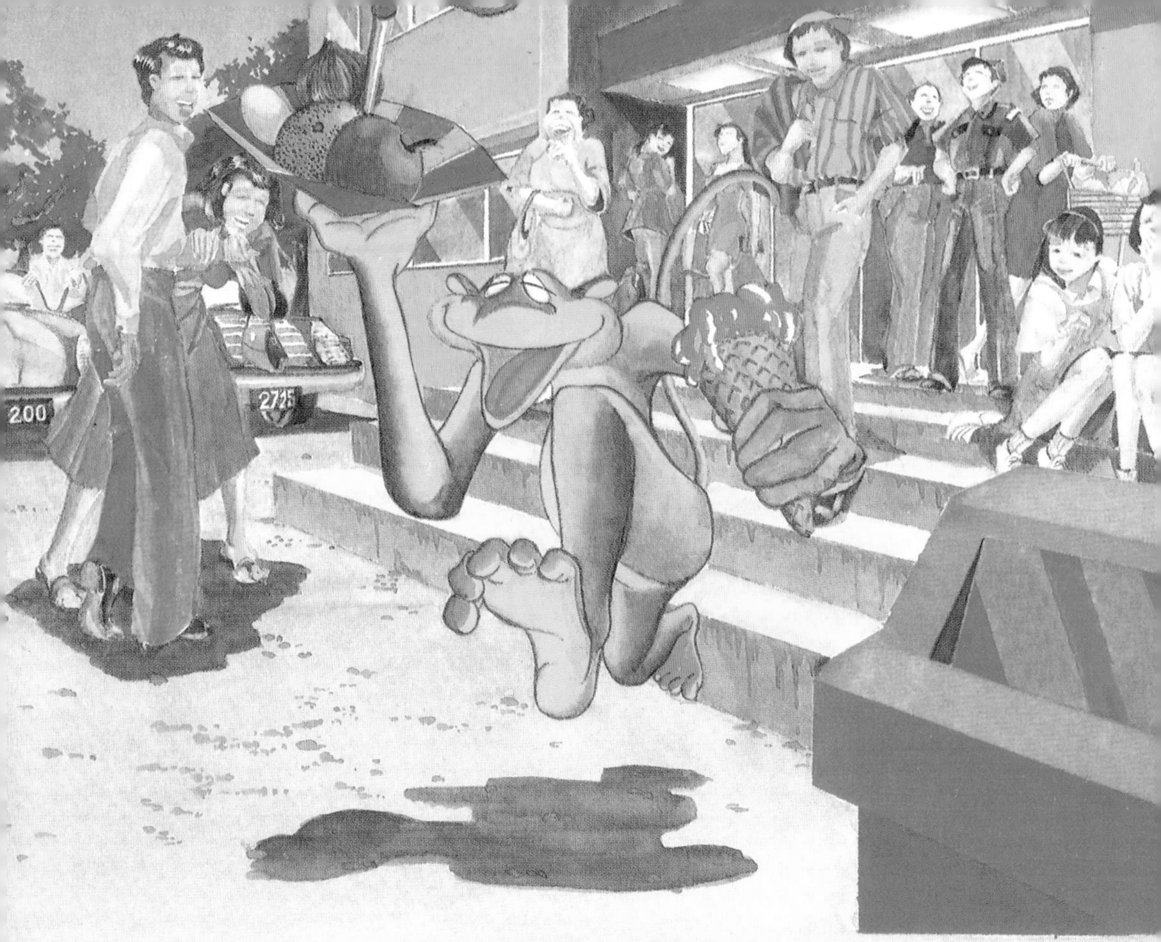

Clever Happy Monkey!